Too Much Clatter!

T0337563

Written by Rob Alcraft

Illustrated by Rachael and Phillippa Corcutt

Collins

Miss Green lends me a shell. She says to press it against my ear and I will hear a storm at the coast.

I will hear the wind and the surf thundering too.

But there is too much clatter!
Sterling toots a trumpet, and Yasmeen
thumps a drum.

There is too much thump and thwack!
I cannot hear the storm in my shell.

clang

Then at lunch, Sterling crunches crisps,
and Yasmeen slurps and splutters.

There is too much chomp and chatter!
I will never hear the storm in my shell.

On the street, I tell my dad. I press the shell against his ear. Can he hear the storm?

vroom

bleep

Dad shrugs. He just hears the street!
He cannot hear a storm in my shell.

Dad gets us a snack, but I get cross!
My shell has been stuffed with toast.

I scrub my shell, but I am in a grump!
I will never hear that storm.

I am still upset when I go to bed. Then I see my shell, smooth and glimmering.

I hear the storm, far off. I hear the wind, and I drift off to sleep.

The storm in the shell

🐾 Review: After reading 🐾

Use your assessment from hearing the children read to choose any GPCs, words or tricky words that need additional practice.

Read 1: Decoding

- Turn to page 12 and point to the word **glimmering**. Ask the children to read pages 11 and 12 to check its meaning. Ask:
  - o What is it describing? (*the shell*) What did the boy do with his shell on page 11? (*scrub/wash it*)
  - o What do you think a clean shell looks like? (e.g. *shiny, gleaming*) Discuss whether the children had guessed that **glimmering** means, for example "shining".
- Ask the children to read these words. Check that they sound out all the adjacent consonants.

  toast   **screech**   **against**   **storm**   **vroom**   **splutters**

- On pages 4 and 5, point to the sound words in turn. Say: Can you blend in your head when you read these words?

Read 2: Prosody

- Model reading page 8, emphasising the sound words. Point out how you used a high electronic tone for **bleep**, and a deeper engine tone for **vroom**.
- Challenge the children to read page 9. Say: Can you make the words in the picture sound like car brakes and a dog?

Read 3: Comprehension

- Ask the children if they have found a noise or noises too loud. What sort of noises were they? Where were they?
- Discuss why the clatter was a problem for the boy. Ask: What quieter sound could he not hear? Do you think it's important to be able to hear quieter sounds sometimes? Why?
- Ask the children what other people in the story could have done to help? Encourage them to consider how it can help for people to have somewhere quieter to go when noise becomes too overwhelming.
- Ask the children to retell the story using the pictures on pages 14 and 15 as prompts. Children can take turns telling the events in each picture. Open out to the group by asking:
  - o What was the clatter at this stage in the story? Can you say the sound words?
  - o How was the boy feeling at this point? Why?